WILDLIFE SANCTUARIES

New Hampshire Ecoregions

Northeastern Highlands
Northeastern Coastal Zone

1. Connecticut Lakes State Forest
2. Lake Francis Wildlife Area
3. Umbagog National Wildlife Refuge
4. Fort Hill Wildlife
5. Twin Mountain Fish Hatchery
6. Warren Fish & Wildlife Center
7. Paradise Point Nature Center
8. Squam Lakes Natural Science Center
9. The Loon Center
10. Harris Center for Conservation Education
11. Woodman Institute Museum
12. Great Bay Discovery Center
13. Seacoast Science Center
14. Bear Brook State Park
15. Massabesic Audubon Center
16. Beaver Brook Association
17. Wapack National Wildlife Refuge
18. McLane Audubon Center
19. Pondicherry Wildlife Refuge
20. Cardigan Mountain State Park
21. Prescott Farm Environmental Education Center
22. John Hay National Wildlife Refuge
23. Helen Woodruff Smith Bird Sanctuary
24. Margret & H.A. Rey Center

NEW HAMPSHIRE WILDLIFE

A Folding Pocket Guide to Familiar Animals

INVERTEBRATES

Spiny Sun Star
Crossaster papposus
To 14 in. (35 cm)

Sand Dollar
Echinarachnius parma
To 3 in. (8 cm)
Skeletons, called 'tests', often wash up on beaches.

Sea Star
Asterias spp.
To 10 in. (13 cm)
Color varies.

Eastern Oyster
Crassostrea virginica
To 10 in. (25 cm)

Northern Quahog
Mercenaria mercenaria
To 5 in. (13 cm)

Knobbed Whelk
Busycon carica
To 9 in. (23 cm)
New Hampshire's state shell.

Blue Crab
Callinectes sapidus
To 9 in. (23 cm)

Horseshoe Crab
Limulus polyphemus
To 12 in. (30 cm) wide.

Blue Mussel
Mytilus edulis
To 4 in. (10 cm)

Nine-spotted Lady Beetle
Coccinella novemnotata
To .25 in. (.6 cm)
New Hampshire's state insect.

Black-and-yellow Garden Spider
Argiope aurantia
To 1.25 in. (3.2 cm)

Northern Lobster
Homarus americanus
To 3 ft. (90 cm)

Ebony Jewelwing
Calopteryx maculata
To 1.75 in. (4.5 cm)
Like most damselflies, it rests with its wings held together over its back.

Green Darner
Anax junius
To 3 in. (8 cm)
Like most dragonflies, it rests with its wings open.

Cicada
Tibicen spp.
To 1.5 in. (4 cm)
Song is a sudden loud whine or buzz, maintained steadily before dying away.

Field Cricket
Gryllus pennsylvanicus
To 1 in. (3 cm)
Song is a series of three chirps.

BUTTERFLIES & MOTHS

Spring Azure
Celastrina ladon
To 1.3 in. (3.6 cm)
One of the earliest spring butterflies.

Question Mark
Polygonia interrogationis
To 3 in. (5 cm)
Note lilac margin on wings. Silvery mark on underwings resembles a question mark or semicolon.

Baltimore Checkerspot
Euphydryas phaeton
To 2.5 in. (6 cm)

Red Admiral
Vanessa atalanta
To 2.5 in. (6 cm)

American Copper
Lycaena phlaeas
To 1.25 in. (3.2 cm)

Viceroy
Limenitis archippus
To 3 in. (8 cm)
Told from similar monarch by its smaller size and the thin, black band on its hindwings.

Karner Blue Butterfly
Lycaeides melissa
To 1.3 in. (3.3 cm)
New Hampshire's state butterfly.

Monarch
Danaus plexippus
To 4 in. (10 cm)

Eastern Tiger Swallowtail
Papilio glaucus
To 6 in. (15 cm)

Mourning Cloak
Nymphalis antiopa
To 3.5 in. (9 cm)
Emerges during the first spring thaw.

Cecropia Silkmoth
Hyalophora cecropia
To 6 in. (15 cm)
Note white, crescent-shaped marks on hindwings.

Hummingbird Clearwing
Hemaris thysbe
To 2 in. (5 cm)
Wings have clear patches. Hovers near flowers like a hummingbird.

Eight-Spotted Forester
Alypia octomaculata
To 1 in. (3 cm)
Active during the day.

Luna Moth
Actias luna
To 4.5 in. (11 cm)

Woolly Bear Caterpillar

Monarch Caterpillar

FISHES

Rainbow Trout
Oncorhynchus mykiss To 44 in. (1.1 m)
Note reddish side stripe.

Lake Trout
Salvelinus namaycush To 4 ft. (1.2 m)
Dark fish is covered in light spots. Tail is deeply forked.

Lake Whitefish
Coregonus clupeaformis
To 30 in. (75 cm)
Note concave forehead.

Brook Trout
Salvelinus fontinalis To 28 in. (70 cm)
Reddish side spots have blue halos.
New Hampshire's state freshwater fish.

Pumpkinseed
Lepomis gibbosus To 16 in. (40 cm)

Largemouth Bass
Micropterus salmoides To 40 in. (1 m)
Note prominent side spots. Jaw joint extends past eye.

Crappie
Pomoxis spp. To 16 in. (40 cm)
Note humped back.

Smallmouth Bass
Micropterus dolomieu To 27 in. (68 cm)
Jaw joint is beneath the eye.

Bluegill
Lepomis macrochirus To 16 in. (40 cm)

Striped Bass
Morone saxatilis To 6 ft. (1.8 m)
Has 6-9 dark side stripes.
New Hampshire's state saltwater fish.

Chain Pickerel
Esox niger To 31 in. (78 cm)
Has chain-like pattern on sides.

Yellow Perch
Perca flavescens To 16 in. (40 cm)
Note 6-9 dark 'saddles' down its side.

Winter Flounder
Pseudopleuronectes americanus
To 2 ft. (60 cm)

Bluefish
Pomatomus saltatrix To 43 in. (1.1 m)
Short first dorsal fin has 7-8 spines.

REPTILES & AMPHIBIANS

Spring Peeper
Pseudacris crucifer
To 1.5 in. (4 cm)
Note dark X on back. Musical call is a series of short peeps.

Bullfrog
Lithobates catesbeianus
To 8 in. (20 cm)
Call is a deep-pitched – jug-o-rum.

American Toad
Anaxyrus americanus
To 4.5 in. (11 cm)
Call is a high musical trill lasting up to 30 seconds.

Northern Leopard Frog
Lithobates pipiens
To 4.5 in. (11 cm)
Brown to green frog has dark spots on its back. Call is a rattling snore with grunts and moans.

Wood Frog
Lithobates sylvaticus
To 3 in. (8 cm)
Note dark mask. Staccato call is duck-like.

Green Frog
Lithobates clamitans
To 4 in. (10 cm)
Single-note call is a banjo-like twang.

Eastern Painted Turtle
Chrysemys picta picta To 10 in. (25 cm)
Note red marks on outer edge of shell.

Red-spotted Newt
Notophthalmus viridescens
To 6 in. (15 cm)
New Hampshire's state amphibian.

Snapping Turtle
Chelydra serpentina To 18 in. (45 cm)
Note knobby shell and long tail.

Red Eft
Juvenile form of a red-spotted newt.

Common Garter Snake
Thamnophis sirtalis sirtalis To 4 ft. (1.2 m)
Brownish snake has yellowish back stripes.

Milk Snake
Lampropeltis triangulum triangulum
To 7 ft. (2.1 m)

Northern Water Snake
Nerodia sipedon To 4.5 ft. (1.4 m)
Note dark blotches on back.

Smooth Green Snake
Opheodrys vernalis
To 26 in. (65 cm)

Eastern Ribbon Snake
Thamnophis sauritus sauritus
To 40 in. (1 m)
Slender snake has 3 distinct stripes.

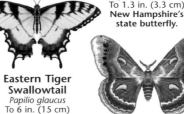

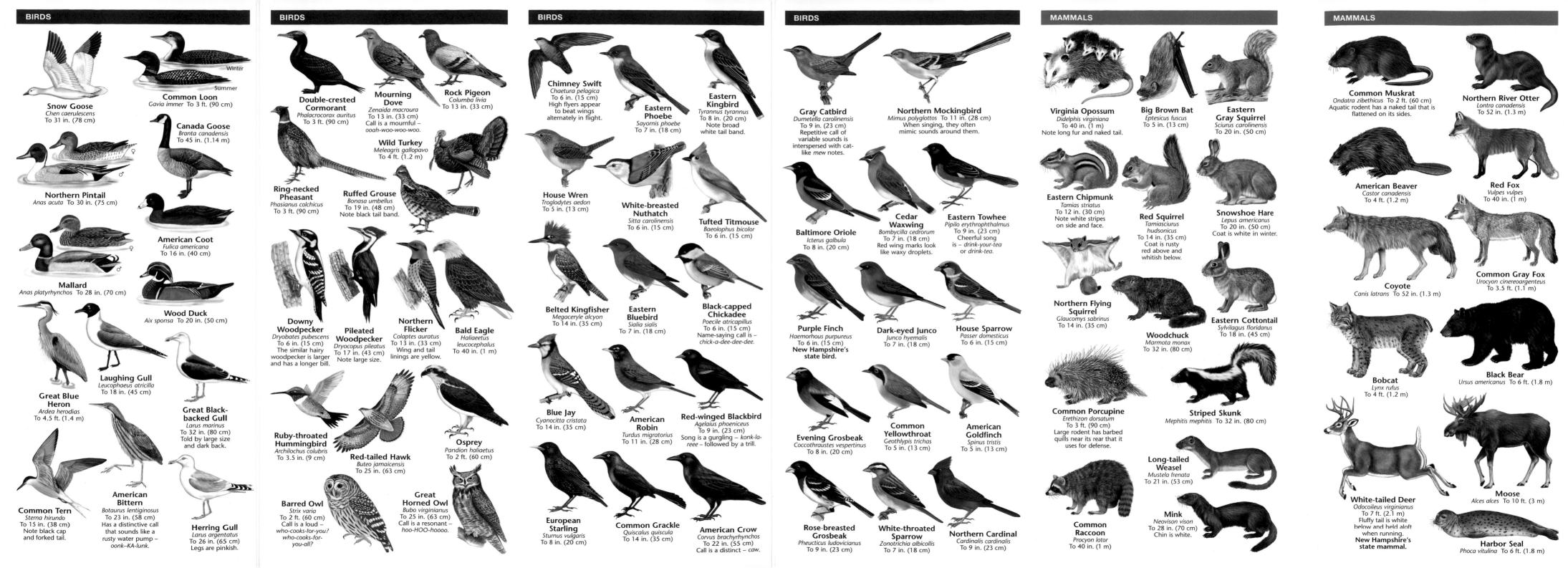

BIRDS

Snow Goose
Chen caerulescens
To 31 in. (78 cm)

Common Loon
Gavia immer To 3 ft. (90 cm)
Winter
Summer

Canada Goose
Branta canadensis
To 45 in. (1.14 m)

Northern Pintail
Anas acuta To 30 in. (75 cm) ♂

American Coot
Fulica americana
To 16 in. (40 cm)

Mallard
Anas platyrhynchos To 28 in. (70 cm) ♀ ♂

Wood Duck
Aix sponsa To 20 in. (50 cm)

Great Blue Heron
Ardea herodias
To 4.5 ft. (1.4 m)

Laughing Gull
Leucophaeus atricilla
To 18 in. (45 cm)

Great Black-backed Gull
Larus marinus
To 32 in. (80 cm)
Told by large size
and dark back.

Common Tern
Sterna hirundo
To 15 in. (38 cm)
Note black cap
and forked tail.

American Bittern
Botaurus lentiginosus
To 23 in. (58 cm)
Has a distinctive call
that sounds like a
rusty water pump –
oonk–KA–lunk.

Herring Gull
Larus argentatus
To 26 in. (65 cm)
Legs are pinkish.

BIRDS

Double-crested Cormorant
Phalacrocorax auritus
To 3 ft. (90 cm)

Mourning Dove
Zenaida macroura
To 13 in. (33 cm)
Call is a mournful –
ooah-woo-woo-woo.

Rock Pigeon
Columba livia
To 13 in. (33 cm)

Wild Turkey
Meleagris gallopavo
To 4 ft. (1.2 m)

Ring-necked Pheasant
Phasianus colchicus
To 3 ft. (90 cm)

Ruffed Grouse
Bonasa umbellus
To 19 in. (48 cm)
Note black tail band.

Downy Woodpecker
Dryobates pubescens
To 6 in. (15 cm)
The similar hairy
woodpecker is larger
and has a longer bill.

Pileated Woodpecker
Dryocopus pileatus
To 17 in. (43 cm)
Note large size.

Northern Flicker
Colaptes auratus
To 13 in. (33 cm)
Wing and tail
linings are yellow.

Bald Eagle
Haliaeetus leucocephalus
To 40 in. (1 m)

Ruby-throated Hummingbird
Archilochus colubris
To 3.5 in. (9 cm)

Red-tailed Hawk
Buteo jamaicensis
To 25 in. (63 cm)

Osprey
Pandion haliaetus
To 2 ft. (60 cm)

Barred Owl
Strix varia
To 2 ft. (60 cm)
Call is a loud –
who-cooks-for-you?
who-cooks-for-
you-all?

Great Horned Owl
Bubo virginianus
To 25 in. (63 cm)
Call is a resonant –
hoo-HOO-hoooo.

BIRDS

Chimney Swift
Chaetura pelagica
To 6 in. (15 cm)
High flyers appear
to beat wings
alternately in flight.

Eastern Phoebe
Sayornis phoebe
To 7 in. (18 cm)

Eastern Kingbird
Tyrannus tyrannus
To 8 in. (20 cm)
Note broad
white tail band.

House Wren
Troglodytes aedon
To 5 in. (13 cm)

White-breasted Nuthatch
Sitta carolinensis
To 6 in. (15 cm)

Tufted Titmouse
Baeolophus bicolor
To 6 in. (15 cm)

Belted Kingfisher
Megaceryle alcyon
To 14 in. (35 cm)

Eastern Bluebird
Sialia sialis
To 7 in. (18 cm)

Black-capped Chickadee
Poecile atricapillus
To 6 in. (15 cm)
Name-saying call is –
chick-a-dee-dee-dee.

Blue Jay
Cyanocitta cristata
To 14 in. (35 cm)

American Robin
Turdus migratorius
To 11 in. (28 cm)

Red-winged Blackbird
Agelaius phoeniceus
To 9 in. (23 cm)
Song is a gurgling – konk-la-
reee – followed by a trill.

European Starling
Sturnus vulgaris
To 8 in. (20 cm)

Common Grackle
Quiscalus quiscula
To 14 in. (35 cm)

American Crow
Corvus brachyrhynchos
To 22 in. (55 cm)
Call is a distinct – caw.

BIRDS

Gray Catbird
Dumetella carolinensis
To 9 in. (23 cm)
Repetitive call of
variable sounds is
interspersed with cat-
like mew notes.

Northern Mockingbird
Mimus polyglottos To 11 in. (28 cm)
When singing, they often
mimic sounds around them.

Baltimore Oriole
Icterus galbula
To 8 in. (20 cm)

Cedar Waxwing
Bombycilla cedrorum
To 7 in. (18 cm)
Red wing marks look
like waxy droplets.

Eastern Towhee
Pipilo erythrophthalmus
To 9 in. (23 cm)
Cheerful song
is – drink-your-tea
or drink-tea.

Purple Finch
Haemorhous purpureus
To 6 in. (15 cm)
**New Hampshire's
state bird.**

Dark-eyed Junco
Junco hyemalis
To 7 in. (18 cm)

House Sparrow
Passer domesticus
To 6 in. (15 cm)

Evening Grosbeak
Coccothraustes vespertinus
To 8 in. (20 cm)

Common Yellowthroat
Geothlypis trichas
To 5 in. (13 cm)

American Goldfinch
Spinus tristis
To 5 in. (13 cm)

Rose-breasted Grosbeak
Pheucticus ludovicianus
To 9 in. (23 cm)

White-throated Sparrow
Zonotrichia albicollis
To 7 in. (18 cm)

Northern Cardinal
Cardinalis cardinalis
To 9 in. (23 cm)

MAMMALS

Virginia Opossum
Didelphis virginiana
To 40 in. (1 m)
Note long fur and naked tail.

Big Brown Bat
Eptesicus fuscus
To 5 in. (13 cm)

Eastern Gray Squirrel
Sciurus carolinensis
To 20 in. (50 cm)

Eastern Chipmunk
Tamias striatus
To 12 in. (30 cm)
Note white stripes
on side and face.

Red Squirrel
Tamiasciurus hudsonicus
To 14 in. (35 cm)
Coat is rusty
red above and
whitish below.

Snowshoe Hare
Lepus americanus
To 20 in. (50 cm)
Coat is white in winter.

Northern Flying Squirrel
Glaucomys sabrinus
To 14 in. (35 cm)

Woodchuck
Marmota monax
To 32 in. (80 cm)

Eastern Cottontail
Sylvilagus floridanus
To 18 in. (45 cm)

Common Porcupine
Erethizon dorsatum
To 3 ft. (90 cm)
Large rodent has barbed
quills near its rear that it
uses for defense.

Striped Skunk
Mephitis mephitis To 32 in. (80 cm)

Long-tailed Weasel
Mustela frenata
To 21 in. (53 cm)

Common Raccoon
Procyon lotor
To 40 in. (1 m)

Mink
Neovison vison
To 28 in. (70 cm)
Chin is white.

MAMMALS

Common Muskrat
Ondatra zibethicus To 2 ft. (60 cm)
Aquatic rodent has a naked tail that is
flattened on its sides.

Northern River Otter
Lontra canadensis
To 52 in. (1.3 m)

American Beaver
Castor canadensis
To 4 ft. (1.2 m)

Red Fox
Vulpes vulpes
To 40 in. (1 m)

Coyote
Canis latrans To 52 in. (1.3 m)

Common Gray Fox
Urocyon cinereoargenteus
To 3.5 ft. (1.1 m)

Bobcat
Lynx rufus
To 4 ft. (1.2 m)

Black Bear
Ursus americanus To 6 ft. (1.8 m)

White-tailed Deer
Odocoileus virginianus
To 7 ft. (2.1 m)
Fluffy tail is white
below and held aloft
when running.
**New Hampshire's
state mammal.**

Moose
Alces alces To 10 ft. (3 m)

Harbor Seal
Phoca vitulina To 6 ft. (1.8 m)